M000073582

CHOWAN BEACH

CHOWAN BEACH

Remembering an
African American Resort

FRANK STEPHENSON

Charleston · London

History
PRESS

Published by The History Press
Charleston, SC 29403
www.historypress.net

Copyright © 2006 by Frank Stephenson
All rights reserved

Cover Image: African Americans during segregation and the Jim Crow years turned to Chowan Beach for rest, fun and relaxation, as seen in this July 1958 photo. *Frank Stephenson Photo Archives.*

First published 2006

ISBN 978-1-5402-2478-1

Library of Congress Cataloging-in-Publication Data

Stephenson, E. Frank.
Chowan Beach : remembering an African American resort / Frank Stephenson.
p. cm.
ISBN 1-59629-164-8 (alk. paper)
1. Chowan Beach (N.C.)--History. 2. Summer resorts--North Carolina--Chowan Beach--History. 3. Chowan Beach (N.C.)--History--Pictorial works. 4. Chowan Beach (N.C.)--Social life and customs. 5. Chowan Beach (N.C.)--Biography. 6. African Americans--North Carolina--Chowan Beach--History. 7. African Americans--North Carolina--Chowan Beach--Social life and customs. 8. African Americans--North Carolina--Chowan Beach--Biography. I. Title.
F264.C45S74 2006
975.6'153--dc22

2006021095

Notice: The information in this book is true and complete to the best of our knowledge. It is offered without guarantee on the part of the author or The History Press. The author and The History Press disclaim all liability in connection with the use of this book.
All rights reserved. No part of this book may be reproduced or transmitted in any form whatsoever without prior written permission from the publisher except in the case of brief quotations embodied in critical articles and reviews.

Spend Your Vacation At

CHOWAN
BEACH

WHICH OPENS
MEMORIAL
DAY, MAY 30

Here's the summer resort that has everything! Nestling amid the luxurious foliage and towering trees, which form a veritable canopy over the resort, of North Carolina rests Chowan Beach. It is truly a "Fountain of Youth." For tired worn out nerves it has no equal. FISH, SWIM, CANOE or bask in the healing sun rays of this incomparable beach and you will find new vigor, new life.

Here you will find large comfortable rooms and cottages equipped with hot and cold running water, shower baths and electric lights. Our dining room is unexcelled for its fine, wholesome food at prices everyone can afford. Free Picnic Sheds, Swings, Beach Benches, Dressing Rooms for bathing — Parking space for your car.

Chowan Beach

FOR RATES AND RESERVATIONS, WRITE
J. E. REID, Proprietor and Manager

PHONE 35-J   WINTON, N. C.

Mr. Eli Reid, owner and developer of Chowan Beach, advertised frequently in various newspapers. This ad appeared in the May 30, 1936 issue of the *Journal and Guide*, Norfolk, Virginia. *Frank Stephenson Photo Archives.*

CONTENTS

Chowan Beach is located on the banks of the Chowan River in Hertford County in northeastern North Carolina. The nearest town is Winton, which is located about a mile below Chowan Beach on the Chowan River. *Frank Stephenson Photo Archives.*

Acknowledgements

The author gratefully acknowledges with sincere appreciation and deep gratitude for the assistance received from the following that made this book possible:

Mrs. Barbara N. Mulder, Conway, North Carolina
Mrs. Voidy Pillmon, Ahoskie, North Carolina
Ms. Phyllis Pillmon, Ahoskie, North Carolina
Mrs. Keely Jo Pillmon-Holley, Ahoskie, North Carolina
Mrs. Marion Flagg, Washington, D.C.
Mr. Joseph M. Parker, Raleigh, North Carolina
Mrs. Alice Nickens, Winton, North Carolina
Staff, Whitaker Library, Chowan University, Murfreesboro, North Carolina
Staff, Norfolk Public Library, Norfolk, Virginia

INTRODUCTION

Chowan Beach was a four hundred-acre gathering place and vacation destination for African Americans during the segregation era when vacation and beach opportunities were severely limited. This remarkable African American playground began in 1926 with Mr. Eli Reid of Winton and was extended into the early 1990s by Mr. Sam Pillmon of Ahoskie. It was located on the Chowan River a mile above Winton in Hertford County in northeastern North Carolina. Chowan Beach became a major stop on the Chitlin' Circuit as it attracted a whole host of black musicians and headliner performers, including B.B. King, James Brown, Ruth Brown, The Coasters, Joe Turner, Little Willie John, Jimmy Reed, Lance Callaway, Screamin' Jay Hawkins, Carol Drake, Louis Jordan, Clyde McPhatter, the Duke of Earl, Billy Ward and the Dominos, the Orioles, the Ravens, Sam Cooke and the Drifters and numerous others. In its later years following the decline of doo-wop music, "The Beach" became a favorite stop for disco, rhythm and blues and other performers, including Captain Goldie, Freddie King, Eddie Floyd, Blind Man Sam, Ruby Rae Moore, Mable John, Robert Parker, Little Walter, Betty Everett,

(HOWAN BEACH

Daddy Gee, the Kelly Brothers, Amos Milburn, Wildman Steve and more.

Native Americans had occupied this extraordinary site for centuries until displaced by European settlers who began moving into the region in the mid-1600s and very early 1700s. In 1586 Ralph Lane and a group of English colonists from the ill-fated Roanoke Colony on North Carolina's Outer Banks explored the Chawanook Indian country and the Chowan River north to this site. In 1622 John Pory led an expedition from Jamestown, Virginia, to this region of the Chowan River in search of the 107 men, women and children of the Roanoke Colony who disappeared in 1587 never to be seen again.

Hertford County, North Carolina, had the misfortune of having four villages and towns burn during two wars: two in the American Revolution and two in the Civil War. One of the towns burned in 1862 was its county seat, Winton, when Union troops came up the Chowan River and attacked the town. With the loss of the Hertford County court records in 1862, the early property lineage of Chowan Beach cannot be fully established. We do know that in the 1720s John Gallant operated a ferry here crossing over the Chowan River to Gates County, and Mount Gallant has borne his name ever since because of its high bank. Mount Gallant is shown on several of the very early maps of the region including the 1751 Fry-Jefferson map. The Mount Gallant ferry operated here until the end of the eighteenth century, when it gave way to the competition from the river ferry at Winton, a mile downstream. The Chowan Beach site offers one of the more spectacular views of the peaceful

Chowan River and is located about a mile south of Parker's ferry, one of three river ferries remaining in North Carolina. The Mount Gallant ferry was part of a cluster of river ferries dating back as early as 1710 when Henry Baker had a ferry across the Chowan River at Baker's Point just above Chowan Beach. John Gallant's sister, Penelope, married North Carolina Governor Charles Eden.

Some local legends have placed the notorious pirate Blackbeard here, as it is known that the buccaneer came up the Chowan River as far as Chowan Beach. There has been some speculation that Blackbeard buried his treasure at Chowan Beach, and a number of years ago unknown treasure hunters took that note seriously and attempted to dig it up.

Due to the loss of Hertford County court records—first in 1830 by arsonists and again in 1862 by Union troops—it is impossible to determine the early owners of the Chowan Beach property. It is known that the Vann family of Hertford County had operated a herring seine fishery in Chowan Beach for many years in the early 1800s, and the Jordan family of Winton, North Carolina, acquired the site before the Civil War. The Jordan family retained ownership of the four hundred-acre Mount Gallant or Chowan Beach site until they sold it to Mr. Eli Reid of Winton in 1928. Two years earlier, the Jordan family had leased the Chowan Beach site to Mr. Reid.

One of Mr. Reid's interests in the Chowan Beach site apparently was for its valuable location as a herring seine fishery because of the width of the Chowan River here. The Chowan Beach herring fishing seine was one of the larger herring fishing seines to operate on the upper Chowan River. The seine net was a thousand yards long, twenty feet deep and required twenty men to operate it. In the late 1930s and early 1940s, Mr. Reid teamed up with Mr. Charles L. Revelle of Murfreesboro, North Carolina, to operate this huge herring seine for a few years. Prior to his death in 1996, Mr. Revelle pleasantly recalled his days of running the Chowan Beach herring seine fishery with Mr. Reid. Mr. Revelle was very fond of Mr. Reid and his herring seine foreman, Mr. John Askew of Winton, who used a sea chantey to inspire the herring seine crew to get the job done. Mr. Revelle remembered one occasion when the seine brought in over one hundred thousand herring in one haul, and it took two days to dip the fish out of the huge net.

In the late 1920s, the genius of Mr. Eli Reid converted one of the abandoned fishing beaches on the Chowan River about a mile north of Winton into one of the more well-known family-oriented resort and playgrounds for African Americans on the East Coast of the United States. Chowan Beach was a place of quiet dignity where African Americans could vacation for a week or two or just visit for the day. In 1967, Mr. Reid sold Chowan Beach to Mr. Sam Pillmon, who was a notable businessman from Ahoskie, North Carolina. Mr. Pillmon made a number of improvements to the resort and it was his astuteness that enabled Chowan Beach to operate into the early 1990s until competition from newly opened amusement parks in neighboring Virginia severely crippled attendance. Although the beach is now closed, the memories made there live on to the present day.

July 4, 1958, view of Chowan Beach near Winton, North Carolina.
Hundreds would enjoy their Independence Day holiday at the beach.
Frank Stephenson Photo Archives.

One Man's Dream
1926-1967

On July 10, 1926, the Jordan family of Winton, North Carolina, leased the Mount Gallant or Chowan Beach property to Mr. J. Eli Reid, a businessman from the same town. The site had been known for years as the location of a major herring fishery, and at that time there were several buildings and boats remaining on the site from that era. On April 5, 1928, Mr. Reid purchased the Chowan Beach property from the Jordan family and owned and operated it for over forty years. Mr. Reid had extensive business interests and was a highly successful distributor of jukeboxes such as Wurlitzer and Rockola, covering eastern North Carolina and parts of neighboring Virginia, including Norfolk. His two daughters, Marion and Gloria, helped their father with collecting coins from the jukeboxes.

It did not take very long for Mr. Reid's dream of turning Chowan Beach into a family-oriented resort or playground for African Americans to take shape. In order for Chowan Beach to become an

attractive vacation site (particularly for black professional families),
Mr. Reid knew that he had to provide excellent accommodations,
top-notch food service and ample safe and clean recreational
activities. His accommodations included family vacation cottages
equipped with electricity and running water, a huge dance hall,
picnic shelters, bathhouses, a large restaurant with public and
private dining facilities, a dormitory-like structure for groups
and a variety of amusement facilities on the beachfront. One
such midway-type piece was a beautiful German-made carousel.
Drinking water for the Chowan Beach facilities came from natural
springs onsite.

On July 30, 1998, Mrs. Marion Reid Flagg, daughter of Mr.
Eli Reid, wrote to Frank Stephenson, "Chowan Beach was a
beautiful place—a place of quiet dignity where people could
come and enjoy themselves. It was the results of my father's
dream of providing a setting, a clean and well-kept one for not
only what we called the picnic crowd (social groups, church
groups, individual families and others), but also for the cottage
guests (a who's who group made up of professionals—doctors,
lawyers, businessmen, college professors...)." Some cottage guests
and their families would vacation at Chowan Beach for several
weeks at a time while others enjoyed a week's stay. Many of the
cottage guests returned year after year and would always request
to stay in their favorite cottage. Mrs. Marion Flagg noted that
many of the cottage guests were outstanding bridge players, and
her father would often borrow card tables for that purpose from
Garrett's funeral home in nearby Ahoskie. Sundays were always

very popular among local folk, often bringing their own picnic spreads and enjoying the whole day. July 4 was always a big day at Chowan Beach, as hundreds would spend their Independence Day holiday there.

Mr. Reid's dream did not disappoint, as Chowan Beach attracted many black professional families from a wide geographic area. The achievements of the families who vacationed there were a testament to the outstanding facilities and family environment that Mr. Reid had fostered and provided his guests. The long list of cottage guests who vacationed at Chowan Beach included bankers, insurance company executives, dentists, medical doctors, surgeons, optometrists, attorneys, business managers, engineers, secondary school educators and college professors from many of the nation's traditional black colleges. Dr. William J. Baudvit, chairman of the math department at Howard University, was one of a number of distinguished professors who with their families vacationed at Chowan Beach. Another internationally famous Howard professor who vacationed at Chowan Beach was Dr. E. Franklin Frazier, who married the daughter of Dr. Calvin S. Brown, founder of Waters Training School in Winton, North Carolina. Chowan Beach also was a favorite vacation site for high-ranking governmental officials from New York, Philadelphia and Washington, D.C.

1950s admission ticket to the dance halls at Chowan Beach. There were two dance halls in use at Chowan Beach, one on the beachfront and an older hall on the hill. *Frank Stephenson Photo Archives.*

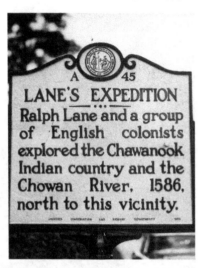

In 1586 Ralph Lane and a group of English colonists from the ill-fated Roanoke Colony on North Carolina's Outer Banks explored the Chowanook Indian country and the Chowan River north of the Chowan Beach site. *Frank Stephenson Photo Archives.*

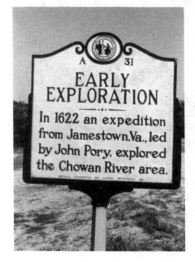

In 1622 John Pory led an expedition from Jamestown, Virginia, to the Chowan Beach region in search of the 107 men, women and children of the Roanoke Colony who disappeared in 1587. *Frank Stephenson Photo Archives.*

21

Chowan Beach sits on the west bank of North Carolina's magnificent Chowan River in Hertford County. The river is an interstate stream that is formed by the confluence of the Blackwater and Nottoway Rivers at the Virginia–North Carolina state line. It follows a southeasterly path for over fifty miles before it joins the Albemarle Sound near Edenton, North Carolina. *Frank Stephenson Photo Archives.*

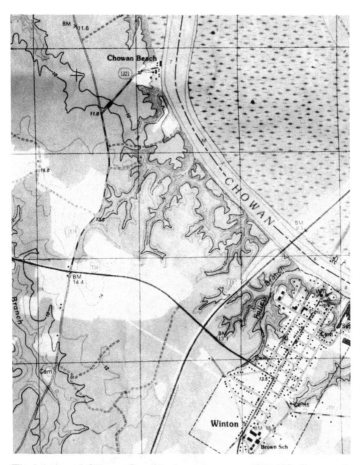

The location of Chowan Beach is shown here on a 1982 U.S. Coast and Geodetic Survey map of Winton, North Carolina. Winton is located approximately a mile below Chowan Beach on the Chowan River. *Frank Stephenson Photo Archives*.

Chowan Beach

Road sign for the Chowan Beach or North Carolina state secondary road 1321 that branches off Parker's Ferry Road (state secondary road 1175). This road connects to U.S. 158. When the Chowan Beach property was sold in 2004, the new owners petitioned the Hertford County Board of Commissioners to declare that the road was no longer a part of the state secondary road system. Today the road is a gated private road. *Frank Stephenson Photo Archives.*

J. Eli Reid was born in Hertford County, North Carolina, on December 13, 1887, and died on July 27, 1971. Mr. Reid was a World War I veteran, trustee of First Baptist Church of Winton and owner and operator of Chowan Beach for forty-one years. *Courtesy of Mrs. Marion Reid Flagg*

It's Vacation Time at - - -

CHOWAN BEACH

North Carolina's Fountain of Youth

● ●

Come Down. Spend a Restful and Invigorating Vacation. Beautiful Shade Trees, Natural Spring Water, Cozy Cottages. Equipped With Hot and Cold Running Water, and Unsurpassed Food. Prices Reasonable.

BOOK YOUR PICNICS NOW!
SAFE SWIMMING
FISHERMEN'S PARADISE
SPECIAL WEEK-END RATES

For Reservations. Phone or Write

J. E. REID

Proprietor-Manager

Phone 35-1   Winton, N. C.

Advertisement appearing in the June 22, 1935 issue of the *Journal and Guide. Frank Stephenson Photo Archives.*

1930s postcard featuring activity images of Chowan Beach. *Courtesy of Mrs. Marion Reid Flagg.*

Advertisement appearing in the August 13, 1935 issue of the *Journal and Guide*. Frank Stephenson Photo Archives.

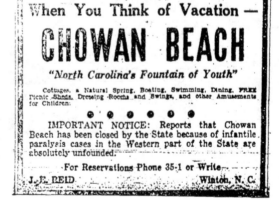

When You Think of Vacation —

CHOWAN BEACH

"North Carolina's Fountain of Youth"

Cottages, a Natural Spring, Boating, Swimming, Dining, FREE Picnic Sheds, Dressing Rooms and Swings, and other Amusements for Children.

IMPORTANT NOTICE: Reports that Chowan Beach has been closed by the State because of infantile paralysis cases in the Western part of the State are absolutely unfounded.

For Reservations Phone 35-1 or Write

J. E. REID   Winton, N. C.

FOURTH ANNUAL CELEBRATION
of CHOWAN BEACH

Monday and Monday Night, August 19

DANCING - BOTH AFTERNOON AND NIGHT - UNTIL ???? O'CLOCK.
MUSIC AT NIGHT BY PUFF AND NOLMAN'S CAROLINIANS OF ELIZA-
BETH CITY. SURF BATHING - BOAT RIDING - MERRY-GO-ROU'
AND OTHER AMUSEMENTS. COME AND ENJOY THE DAY A
NIGHT.
J. ELEY REID, Proprietor and Manager

Advertisement appearing in the August 17, 1929 issue of the *Journal and Guide*. *Frank Stephenson Photo Archives.*

Chowan Beach
On The Picturesque
Chowan River. Winton. N. C.

BATHING—BOATING—FISHING—DINING—DANCING
INDIVIDUAL COTTAGES FOR VACATIONISTS
IDEAL FOR CHURCH, SOCIETY OR PRIVATE PICNICS. WRITE
J. E. REID, Winton, N. C.

Advertisement appearing in the June 6, 1931 issue of the *Journal and Guide*. *Frank Stephenson Photo Archives.*

CHOWAN BEACH

J. E. REID, Proprietor

WINTON, N. C.

Meals Served

European Plan

HOT AND COLD RUNNING WATER

● Fishing

● Bathing

● Dancing

● Cottages

SHOWER BATHS

Advertisement appearing in the August 13, 1935 issue of the *Journal and Guide*. *Frank Stephenson Photo Archives.*

Welcome to CHOWAN BEACH

1½ Miles West of Winton on the Beautiful Chowan River

FOR COMPLETE SUMMER ENTERTAINMENT

❖ RIDES
❖ FUN HOUSE
❖ DANCING
❖ BOATING
❖ COTTAGES

❖ PICNIC SHED and TABLES
❖ Natural Spring Water
❖ NO CHARGE for Use of Bath House

J. E. REID Proprietor **Winton, N.C.**

Undated advertisement probably from the *Hertford County Herald*, Ahoskie, North Carolina. *Frank Stephenson Photo Archives.*

It's Vacation
Time at

CHOWAN
BEACH

"North Carolina's Fountain of Youth"

Spend A Grand And Glorious

4TH OF JULY

HERE

Boating, Swimming, Dining, FREE Picnic Sheds, Free Dressing Rooms, Free Swings and other Amusements for Children.

For reservations Phone 35-1 or Write

J. E. REID   Winton, N. C.

Advertisement appearing in the June 29, 1935 issue of the *Journal and Guide. Frank Stephenson Photo Archives.*

Advertisement appearing in the July 4, 1936 issue of the *Journal and Guide*. *Frank Stephenson Photo Archives.*

Advertisement appearing in the May 29, 1937 issue of the *Journal and Guide*, Norfolk, Virginia. *Frank Stephenson Photo Archives.*

CHOWAN BEACH

Finest Summering Place South for Colored Folk

On the Picturesque Chowan River at Winton, N. C.

Magnificent Scenery. Fine Bathing. Boating and Fishing---Elegantly appointed Individual Cottages for vacationists, Fine Dance Pavilion. First Class Cafeteria. Best Roads, Splendid Surrounding Country and People---Cool, Quiet, Restful and Health-Giving.

Ideal for Church, Society, Private or Public Picnics

Easily accessible to all points in Eastern North Carolina and Tidewater Virginia, offering thousands of motorists an opportunity to spend the week-end or Sunday during the hot summer months where they can have comfort and enjoyment at the minimum expense. Reservations are now open; rates are surprisingly low. Write for further information to

J. E. REID, Winton, N. C.

 Drive to Chowan Beach

Take either of Two Routes:—Suffolk to Sunbury—To Winton, or Franklin to Murfreesboro, to Winton. Spend a day or week. Give the Family an Outing.

Advertisement appearing in the May 30, 1931 issue of the *Journal and Guide. Frank Stephenson Photo Archives.*

CHOWAN BEACH

Two visitors from Durham, North Carolina, enjoying a wade in the Chowan River at Chowan Beach. *Courtesy of Mrs. Marion Reid Flagg.*

1930s view of the Chowan Beach waterfront. *Courtesy of Mrs. Marion Reid Flagg.*

Sisters Marion and Gloria Reid enjoying the beautiful Chowan River at Chowan Beach, 1940s. The two girls practically grew up here. The Reid family would spend their summers at Chowan Beach and the rest of the year at their home in nearby Winton, North Carolina. *Courtesy of Mrs. Marion Reid Flagg.*

Marion and Gloria Reid and their cousin Mary Williamson enjoying a dip in the Chowan River, 1930s. *Courtesy of Mrs. Marion Reid Flagg.*

Gloria Reid and Sallie Weaver sitting on the lawn on the hill overlooking the beachfront, 1940s. *Courtesy of Mrs. Marion Reid Flagg.*

1930s partial view of the Chowan Beach waterfront taken from the hill looking down toward the Chowan River. *Courtesy of Mrs. Marion Reid Flagg*

Mr. and Mrs. J. Eli Reid with their daughters, Marion and Gloria, in the early 1940s. *Courtesy of Mrs. Marion Reid Flagg*

Mrs. Olga Reid, wife of J. Eli Reid, on a boat at Chowan Beach, 1940s. *Courtesy of Mrs. Marion Reid Flagg.*

Carolina's Finest Resort For Negroes

Chowan Beach

WINTON, N. C.

On the Beautiful and Historic Chowan River

Bathing - Boating - Dancing

Amid Pleasant Surroundings and Beautiful Scenery

MODERN, COMFORTABLE COTTAGES

Herring Fishery

In the early spring each year, when from the ocean the delectable shad and the succulent herring seek the placid waters of the Chowan and its tributary creeks in great numbers for spawning, here at Chowan Beach is operated one of the largest fisheries in North Carolina. Modern equipment and careful handling of the catches combine to make this one of Hertford County's important industries. Known historically as the old Mt. Gallant Fishery—where before the war slaves pulled the oars of the boats that "shot" the great seines—the fishery is now operated each season by J. Eley Reid and his associate under the trade name of Mt. Gallant Fishery Company.

Auto Service

Filling station and repair service of the highest type. . . Where the needs of motorists, white and colored, receive courteous, speedy, dependable attention in every detail. . . Good Gulf Gasoline and Oils. Complete, Modern Equipment.

REID'S SERVICE STATION
On the Highway At Junction Routes No. 35 and 35

J. E. REID, Owner and Manager

WINTON, NORTH CAROLINA

Advertisement appearing in the August 17, 1939 issue of the *Hertford County Herald*, Ahoskie, North Carolina. *Frank Stephenson Photo Archives.*

37

Marion and Gloria Reid and friends enjoying a picnic on the waterfront at Chowan Beach, 1945. *Courtesy of Mrs. Marion Reid Flagg.*

View of the boat ramp at Chowan Beach, not dated. *Courtesy of Mrs. Marion Reid Flagg*

The Pepsi delivery truck driver who made weekly stops at Chowan Beach, not dated. *Courtesy of Mrs. Marion Reid Flagg*

Marion and Gloria Reid on the waterfront, 1945. *Courtesy of Mrs. Marion Reid Flagg.*

Marion and Gloria Reid and cousin Helen James on the beachfront, 1945. *Courtesy of Mrs. Marion Reid Flagg.*

Brother and sister Jack and Gloria Reid on the waterfront, 1945. *Courtesy of Mrs. Marion Reid Flagg.*

Photo of sisters Gloria and Marion Reid that appeared in the *Journal and Guide*, not dated. *Courtesy of Mrs. Marion Reid Flagg*

Gloria Reid, 1945. *Courtesy of Mrs. Marion Reid Flagg.*

Undated photo of Mrs. Marion Reid Flagg. *Courtesy of Mrs. Marion Reid Flagg.*

CHOWAN BEACH

The building in Winton, North Carolina, housing Mr. Eli Reid's jukebox and vending machine business in the 1960s. It is now the home of the Town of Winton maintenance department. *Frank Stephenson Photo Archives.*

Some years ago the future of North Carolina's Chowan River was in serious jeopardy of being choked to death by industrial runoff. Today the waters of the Chowan are much clearer, as seen in this view off Chowan Beach. *Frank Stephenson Photo Archives*

One does not have to venture far from Chowan Beach to encounter moss-laden cypress trees and other sights of natural beauty. A number of American bald eagles have been sighted along the Chowan River. *Frank Stephenson Photo Archives*.

Undated view of the original gatehouse at Chowan Beach. *Courtesy of Mrs. Marion Reid Flagg.*

View of the covered picnic shelter on the Chowan Beach waterfront, 1930s. The Reid family summer home is located to the left. *Courtesy of Mrs. Marion Reid Flagg.*

Chowan Beach served as a summer 4-H camp for African American children. In the early 1930s Mr. Reid built this dormitory-like building to house them. *Courtesy of Mrs. Marion Reid Flagg*

The ticket booth for the Chowan Beach carousel, located under the shelter. *Courtesy of Mrs. Marion Reid Flagg*

Chowan Beach

View of the covered picnic area on the waterfront at Chowan Beach, 1940s. *Courtesy of Mrs. Marion Reid Flagg*

Another view of the Reid home on the waterfront at Chowan Beach, 1930s. *Courtesy of Mrs. Marion Reid Flagg.*

View of the bathhouse with sections for male and female patrons, 1930s. *Courtesy of Mrs. Marion Reid Flagg.*

An undated view of the original dance hall at Chowan Beach. It was located on the hill overlooking the Chowan River. James Brown, B.B. King, Ruth Brown, Jimmy Reed, Ivory Joe Hunter and many other famous black entertainers performed in this dance hall. *Courtesy of Mrs. Marion Reid Flagg.*

This building is one of a number of vacation cottages that were available for rent at Chowan Beach. The cottages were equipped with running water and electricity. *Courtesy of Mrs. Marion Reid Flagg.*

Mrs. Olga Reid in an undated photo with her two daughters, Gloria on the left and Marion on the right. *Courtesy of Mrs. Marion Reid Flagg.*

CHOWAN BEACH

View of the waterfront at Chowan Beach featuring the carousel and swing for children, 1960s. *Frank Stephenson Photo Archives.*

View of the fun house and dance hall on the waterfront at Chowan Beach, 1960s. This building was originally built for a herring processing plant by Eli Reid as part of his Mount Gallant herring fishery operation. Mr. Reid converted the building into a dance hall, with the fun house located in the front section of the building. *Frank Stephenson Photo Archives.*

View of the carousel and Chowan Beach waterfront, July 1958. *Frank Stephenson Photo Archives.*

African Americans during segregation and the Jim Crow years turned to Chowan Beach for rest, fun and relaxation, as seen in this July 1958 photo. *Frank Stephenson Photo Archives.*

The German-made carousel was always a big hit at Chowan Beach, as seen in this July 1958 view. *Frank Stephenson Photo Archives.*

An excellent view of the restaurant at Chowan Beach, July 1958. This eatery offered full course meals as well as snacks and sandwiches. There was also a private dining area for cottage guests along with a small photography studio and Mr. Reid's office. *Frank Stephenson Photo Archives.*

Ruth Brown, a native of Portsmouth, Virginia, headlined at Chowan Beach before large crowds a number of times during her very successful career. *Frank Stephenson Photo Archives.*

Chowan Beach was a part of the Chitlin' Circuit, where black musicians
performed for black audiences. This platform paved the way for
top music headliners to perform at Chowan Beach, including Clyde
McPhatter, pictured here. Big Joe Turner, Little Willie John, Mable John,
Al Hibler, Johnny Ace, Earl Grant and many others sang at Chowan
Beach. *Frank Stephenson Photo Archives.*

The grounds at Chowan Beach were always well kept by Mr. Eli Reid, the original owner, and by Mr. Sam Pillmon, the second owner. Both gentlemen maintained a safe family environment all through the years the beach operated. *Frank Stephenson Photo Archives.*

Boat rides were available to the beach's patrons. A boat ramp was attached to the right of the fun house, as seen in this July 1958 view. *Frank Stephenson Photo Archives.*

CHOWAN BEACH

The beautiful shade trees that dotted the landscape at Chowan Beach made it one of the prettiest beaches on the East Coast, as seen in this July 1958 view. *Frank Stephenson Photo Archives.*

The white sands and the sparkling Chowan River waters, July 1958. *Frank Stephenson Photo Archives.*

With natural springs onsite, the crystal clear spring water was always a favorite with Chowan Beach patrons. The small building to the left in this July 1958 photo was the spring house; a small pond is on the right. *Frank Stephenson Photo Archives.*

Church, social and family groups gathered frequently at Chowan Beach. Mrs. Alice Jones Nickens of Winton, North Carolina, took this picture of a family gathering in the late 1940s or early 1950s. *Left to right:* Aunt Cora Jones, Mama Annie Jones, Mrs. Emmce Bouduit of Washington, D.C., Aunt Sallie Jones Eatan and Aunt Kathleen Jones. *Courtesy of Mrs. Alice Jones Nickens.*

CHOWAN BEACH

J. E. REID, Proprietor

Dancing - Boating - Cottages - Refreshments & Sandwiches

Free Parking — Picnic Shed and Tables

Natural Spring Water — No Charge for Use of Bath House

Come and Bring the Family — Give Them a Treat

Located on the Beautiful Chowan River at Winton, N. C.

Follow U. S. Highway 13 to Winton, 1½ Miles West on U. S. 158

Advertisement poster for Chowan Beach probably from the late 1950s. *Frank Stephenson Photo Archives.*

Chowan Beach had its own photography studio where beach patrons could have a keepsake photo made of their visit there. This undated photograph shows Mr. Eli Reid, owner and operator of the beach. *Courtesy of Mrs. Marion Reid Flagg.*

This is an undated poster advertising corned or salted herring for sale at the Mount Gallant Fishery at Chowan Beach. It is believed the poster dates from the early to mid-1930s. *Frank Stephenson Photo Archives.*

II

CHOWAN BEACH AND HERRING FISHING

The alewife or river herring is a migratory fish that spends most of its life in the cold Atlantic Ocean waters off the Canadian Maritime Provinces. Each year in late March, April and May, it returns by the millions to the rivers and creeks of northeastern North Carolina to spawn. For centuries, the people of this region have used various devices—from reed baskets to bow nets, haul seines to pound nets—to catch these silvery saltwater fish. A large haul seine operated at Chowan Beach for many years. Since herring were caught in large numbers, most were salted or corned and fed most of northeastern North Carolina cheaply for over two centuries.

River seines, sometimes called haul or pull seines, were first introduced to the northeastern region of North Carolina in the 1740s by John Campbell, a British navy captain. Campbell sought his fortune in the New World and purchased eight hundred acres of land at Colerain in Bertie County along the Chowan River, approximately twenty miles below Chowan Beach. It was at

(HOWAN BEACH

Herring fishing was a huge endeavor and extremely popular throughout northeastern North Carolina. Chowan Beach had been the home of a large haul seine for many years. This is an 1861 representative drawing of haul seining in the region. *Courtesy of North Carolina Department of Cultural Resources.*

Colerain that John Campbell placed in operation the first seine in North Carolina. It did not take long for this method of herring fishing to become popular. Numerous herring fishing seines, large and small, sprang up along the Chowan River. It is not known exactly when the herring seine was first placed in operation at Chowan Beach, but it is known from the Vann family papers that they operated a herring seine there as early as 1800.

In 1926 when Eli Reid leased the Chowan Beach property, he soon placed in operation a herring seine fishery called Mount Gallant Herring Fishery. In the late 1930s, Charles L. Revelle Sr., a Murfreesboro businessman, became a partner with Mr. Reid in the Mount Gallant Herring Fishery. Their partnership was very successful and continued for a few years into the 1940s. Today the herring still return to the Chowan River region to spawn, but in much smaller numbers. The once-thriving herring fishing industry that prospered along the Chowan River has almost disappeared.

Mt. Gallant Fish Co. Opens as Herring Season Comes in

Good Hauls Are Made First Day

Mt. Gallant Fish Co., located on Chowan River between Winton and Murfreesboro, began operation Wednesday of this week, Chas. L. Revelle informed The News a few days ago.

Prospects are bright for a good herring season, Mr. Revelle said. Hauls form the seine have been comparable to the same time during previous years.

The Mt. Gallant Fish Co. however, experienced some bad luck last week when trying out the seine. One of the motor boats rammed a seine barge and sank. The seine pulled off the barge and was torn by snags when it drifted down stream. Damage was estimated at $100 or more.

The Mt. Gallant Fish Co., one of the oldest fisheries on Chowan River, was put back into operation two years ago by Charles L. Revelle and J. E. Reed. It fell into disuse twenty or more years ago. At one time it was recognized along the eastern seaboard as one of the best in the country.

This story about the Mount Gallant herring seine at Chowan Beach appeared in the March 23, 1939 issue of the *Northeastern North Carolina News*. The Mount Gallant Fish Company was operated for a number of years at Chowan Beach by Charles L. Revelle and Eli Reid. The company utilized one of the largest herring haul seines ever to operate on the upper Chowan River. The seine net was over a thousand yards long, twenty feet deep and required a crew of twenty to operate it. *Frank Stephenson Photo Archives.*

The Mount Gallant Fishery at Chowan Beach was operated by Eli Reid of Winton and Charles L. Revelle Sr., shown here. Mr. Revelle was a businessman from Murfreesboro, North Carolina. *Frank Stephenson Photo Archives.*

John Askew of Winton, North Carolina, was seine master for many years at the Mount Gallant Herring Fishery at Chowan Beach. He would implore his twenty-man haul seine crew to perform their work by employing a chant similar to those used at sea. *Frank Stephenson Photo Archives.*

The saltwater river herring were free for the taking each spring from the rivers and creeks of northeastern North Carolina. Individuals and an untold number of herring fisheries sprang up along the Chowan and Meherrin Rivers, using seines, wire baskets, bow nets and pound nets to catch the alewife by the millions. Many of the fish were consumed locally; others were packed in salt and shipped to different regions. *Frank Stephenson Photo Archives*.

Hundreds of herring that were freshly caught in the Chowan Beach seine await pickup and processing in this early 1930s photo. *Frank Stephenson Photo Archives.*

The herring seine crew at Chowan Beach pulls the huge net on shore in order to dump out the freshly caught fish, early 1930s. *Frank Stephenson Photo Archives.*

The crew loads the huge seine on boats for another sweep across the Chowan River, while on shore another crewmember is shoveling fresh-caught herring into wire baskets, early 1930s. *Frank Stephenson Photo Archives.*

The herring seine at Chowan Beach was no small operation in either manpower or technology, as seen in this remarkable 1941 photo. The herring seine itself was so long and large that it required several boats with inboard motors to pull the heavily laden seine across the Chowan River. *Frank Stephenson Photo Archives.*

71

The pulling of the huge herring seine at Chowan Beach usually attracted a large crowd of onlookers, as seen in this early 1930s photograph. *Frank Stephenson Photo Archives.*

The herring seine crew slowly works the net to shore, early 1940s. The fish will be loaded into a small railroad mining car and pushed into the herring cutting house. *Frank Stephenson Photo Archive.*

This 1941 photograph provides a glimpse inside the herring processing house at Chowan Beach. In later years when the herring seine was no longer in operation, this building was converted into a beachfront dance hall. *Frank Stephenson Photo Archives.*

Members of the herring seine crew are shooting or laying out the huge seine net for another pull across the river. This flat bottom boat was one of eight vessels used in the operation of this large herring seine. *Frank Stephenson Photo Archives.*

Members of the Chowan Beach herring seine crew are seen in this 1941 photograph slowly working the seine toward shore where the catch of fish will be dumped and sorted. *Frank Stephenson Photo Archives.*

Seine master John Askew, *right*, and Charles L. Revelle Sr., *second from right*, are eagerly waiting as the Chowan Beach herring seine is being pulled toward shore for dumping, 1941. *Frank Stephenson Photo Archives.*

Another haul of herring is landed by the Chowan Beach herring seine crew, early 1930s. The building on beach level directly behind the crew is the bathhouse. *Frank Stephenson Photo Archives.*

A gentleman in a boat holds up a section of the Chowan Beach herring seine, 1941. This is required at times when the seine contains a large number of fish: the net begins to sink, causing the fish to escape. *Frank Stephenson Photo Archives.*

1930s view of the Chowan Beach herring seine crew. As many as 100,000 herring have been caught in one sweep across the Chowan River during the peak of the herring season. *Frank Stephenson Photo Archives.*

77

April 1905 photograph of Maddrey's Seine Fishery, which was located on the Meherrin River about six miles from Chowan Beach. *Frank Stephenson Photo Archives.*

Most of the herring seines that operated on the Meherrin and Chowan Rivers were small in comparison to the huge herring seine that operated for many years at Chowan Beach. This small seine was located just above Murfreesboro on the Meherrin River and was operated in the 1960s by Eugene Reid. *Frank Stephenson Photo Archives.*

In the 1920s Paul Jordan operated this small herring seine on the Meherrin River about four miles above Chowan Beach. *Frank Stephenson Photo Archives.*

Herring fishing spawned a way of life and culture that was centered around the return of the herring each spring to northeastern North Carolina. In the creeks where it was impractical to use a seine, other devices were utilized to catch the fish, such as a bow net or dip net, as shown in this view taken at Vaughan's Creek near Murfreesboro, North Carolina. *Frank Stephenson Photo Archives.*

Many of the herring caught on the Chowan and Meherrin Rivers were sold to Perry-Wynns Fish Company in Colerain, North Carolina. The company specialized in corned or salt herring, and many were packed in metal tins like the one pictured here. *Frank Stephenson Photo Archives*.

In 1952, L.D. Perry and Leo Wynns became partners in the world's largest herring processing plant, Perry-Wynns Fish Company, which was located on the west bank of the Chowan River at Colerain, North Carolina. At the peak of the herring fishing season, the company employed about two hundred seasonal workers who cut and salted the fish. In September 2003, Hurricane Isabel sent a wall of water up the Chowan River that destroyed Perry-Wynns Fish Company. *Frank Stephenson Photo Archives*.

A Chowan River herring fisherman unloading his catch at Perry-Wynns Fish Company. The fisherman caught these herring in pound nets he had set on the Chowan River, 1990. *Frank Stephenson Photo Archives.*

After the herring are delivered to Perry-Wynns Fish Company, the fish are sent to the herring cutters where they are cleaned, beheaded and the roe removed. The herring cutter crew was primarily seasonally employed African American women. *Frank Stephenson Photo Archives.*

Herring salting vats at Perry-Wynns Fish Company. Fresh-cut herring are corned or salted down in these huge wooden vats and later packed in jars or bags for market distribution. *Frank Stephenson Photo Archives.*

This cart holds containers of freshly harvested herring roe, considered a delicacy in the northeastern region of North Carolina. The roe is removed to another section of the Perry-Wynns Fish Company, where it is cleaned and canned for market distribution. *Frank Stephenson Photo Archives.*

Herring roe pickers are preparing freshly harvested roe for canning. *Frank Stephenson Photo Archives.*

Perry-Wynns Fish Company used large quantities of salt in the processing of fresh herring. This wheelbarrow was used to transport salt to the huge herring salting vats. *Frank Stephenson Photo Archives.*

The Perry-Wynns Fish Company complex that was located on the Chowan River at Colerain, North Carolina, contained a number of warehouse-like structures. These were destroyed by Hurricane Isabel in September 2003. *Frank Stephenson Photo Archives.*

Tunis Fishery is one of the last remaining herring fisheries in operation on the Chowan River, utilizing pound nets to catch river herring. There were approximately fifty herring fisheries in operation on the Chowan and Meherrin Rivers at the industry's peak years; however, pollution and offshore foreign fishing factories have nearly destroyed herring fishing in northeastern North Carolina. *Frank Stephenson Photo Archives.*

Herring fishing on the Chowan River today has dwindled to a few pound net fishermen, including this crew from Tunis Fishery, located about three miles below Chowan Beach. *Frank Stephenson Photo Archives.*

In the very near future this scene of pound net fishermen on the Chowan River will be no more, as herring fishing in northeastern North Carolina has nearly disappeared. This pound net fishing crew is from Tunis Fishery. *Frank Stephenson Photo Archives.*

This pound net crew from Tunis Fishery uses a small crane to dip herring from one of their pound nets on the Chowan River. *Frank Stephenson Photo Archives.*

The signature device for catching herring in northeastern North Carolina was the haul or pull seine. Giant seines like the one at Chowan Beach were extremely common throughout the area. Unfortunately, in 2006 this haul seine, operated by Williams Fishery on the Meherrin River, is the last operating herring seine in North Carolina. *Frank Stephenson Photo Archives.*

Williams Fishery is located on the Meherrin River in Hertford County, North Carolina, approximately two miles below Murfreesboro. *Frank Stephenson Photo Archives.*

The seine net crew at Williams Fishery. *Frank Stephenson Photo Archives.*

Seine netters from Williams Fishery dump the catch from their last pull. *Frank Stephenson Photo Archives.*

In April 1954 the herring seine crew at Griffith's Fishery, now Williams Fishery, stand knee deep in freshly caught river herring from one sweep across the Meherrin River. *Frank Stephenson Photo Archives.*

This member of the crew at Griffith's Fishery, now Williams Fishery, is seen cleaning fresh herring that were caught in the seine, April 1954. *Frank Stephenson Photo Archives.*

Members of the crew at Williams Fishery are pictured here cleaning freshly caught herring. *Frank Stephenson Photo Archives*

Seine Master Dick Williams and his son Barry are seen repairing the seine at Williams Fishery on the Meherrin River. *Frank Stephenson Photo Archives.*

III

THE SAM PILLMON YEARS
1967-2004

On May 15, 1967, Mr. Sam Pillmon, a highly respected Ahoskie, North Carolina, businessman, purchased Chowan Beach from Mr. Eli Reid. Mr. Pillmon had extensive business holdings in and near Ahoskie including the VIP Club, the VIP Motel, Sam's Café, a vending machine company, rental properties and Sam's Record Shop, which the Pillmon family operated for over forty years.

Mr. Pillmon, following his purchase of Chowan Beach, made a number of improvements including enlarging and bricking the gatehouse, painting and repairing some of the guest cottages and other general maintenance. He expanded the menu in the main restaurant and added concessions on the beachfront. The beach swings, the carousel, the duck pond, the snowball stand and the fun house were always big hits with Chowan Beach patrons. Mr. Pillmon's goal was to make visits to Chowan Beach memorable, rewarding and a good time for all, and he achieved this many times over.

Chowan Beach

When Mr. Pillmon purchased Chowan Beach in 1967, it was changing along with the rest of the country, particularly with respect to music. Disco became the music of choice, and a number of disco performers and other musicians headlined at Chowan Beach during the Pillmon years. Mrs. Voidy Pillmon, widow of Sam Pillmon, recalled a long list of musicians who performed at Chowan Beach: Ruby Rae Moore, Captain Goldie, Mable John, the Kelly Brothers, Freddie King, Wildman Steve, Robert Parker, Betty Everett, Eddie Floyd, Little Willie John, Amos Millburn, Daddy Gee and others. One of the largest crowds ever to attend a music performance at Chowan Beach was for an entertainer named Master Story Teller from Norfolk, Virginia. For a number of years, the beach also hosted church quartets for fantastic gospel music on Sundays.

It is interesting to note that Mrs. Voidy Pillmon's first visit to Chowan Beach was with her 4-H club when she was a young girl growing up in Bertie County, North Carolina. In a 1999 conversation with Frank Stephenson, Mrs. Pillmon recalled her first visit to Chowan Beach and how strange it was that years later she and her husband would purchase the beach from Mr. Reid. The couple operated the beach for over twenty years. In the late 1980s, attendance at Chowan Beach began to fall due to competition from the newly opened theme park King's Dominion in Doswell, Virginia, north of Richmond. In the early 1990s, the Pillmon family sadly closed Chowan Beach, selling the property in 2004. The Pillmon family made the beach a wonderful experience for thousands of patrons who visited there over the years. Chowan Beach was indeed a very special place that was operated by very special people.

Ticket to the fun house at Chowan Beach. The fun house was located in the front end of the beach-level dance hall. *Frank Stephenson Photo Archives.*

The old Mount Gallant ferry road that led to the Chowan River and the beachfront. *Frank Stephenson Photo Archives.*

97

In May 1967, Sam Pillmon, a businessman in Ahoskie, North Carolina, purchased Chowan Beach from Eli Reid. It was Mr. Pillmon's goal to continue the great family atmosphere at Chowan Beach that Mr. Reid had fostered. Mr. Pillmon was born in Colerain, North Carolina, on December 25, 1918, and died in Ahoskie, North Carolina on July 16, 1996. *Courtesy of the Sam Pillmon family.*

May 1972 photograph of Phyllis Pillmon, Beverly Moore and Sam Pillmon on the steps outside the Chowan Beach restaurant. The building in the background is the original dance hall where many headlining African American musicians performed. *Courtesy of the Sam Pillmon family.*

An undated photograph of Ms. Phyllis Pillmon taking a break on the steps outside the Chowan Beach restaurant. *Courtesy of the Sam Pillmon family.*

One of the improvements that Sam Pillmon made was to enlarge and brick up the gatehouse. *Frank Stephenson Photo Archives.*

One of many social and family gatherings held at Chowan Beach. This particular event was held was held on July 2, 1972, and celebrated the seventy-sixth birthday of Mrs. Ora Pillmon, mother of Mr. Sam Pillmon. *Courtesy of the Sam Pillmon family.*

Mrs. Ora Pillmon's seventy-sixth birthday celebration. *Courtesy of the Sam Pillmon family.*

Mrs. Suzie Pillman Roulhac, sister of Mr. Sam Pillmon, was responsible for arranging bus trips from Washington, D.C., to Chowan Beach. *Courtesy of the Sam Pillmon family.*

Freddie Reynolds was a longtime caretaker at Chowan Beach. *Courtesy of the Sam Pillmon family.*

Ms. Kelly Jo Pillmon-Holley enjoying a walk on the lawn at Chowan Beach. *Courtesy of the Sam Pillmon family.*

Ms. Phyllis Pillmon, Ms. Arthelia Parker and Ms. Kelly Jo Pillmon in front of the duck pond on the waterfront at Chowan Beach. *Courtesy of the Sam Pillmon family.*

CHOWAN BEACH

Undated photograph of Ms. Phyllis Pillmon in front of one of the guest cottages. *Courtesy of the Sam Pillmon family.*

Undated photograph of Ms. Annie Mae Pillmon, sister of Mr. Sam Pillmon, on the steps leading to the beachfront. *Courtesy of the Sam Pillmon family.*

Mrs. Voidy Pillmon worked side by side with her husband Sam to make Chowan Beach one of the best-known African American playgrounds and amusement parks on the East Coast. *Courtesy of the Sam Pillmon family.*

Ms. Arthelia Parker and Ms. Kelly Jo Pillmon in front of one of the guest cottages. *Courtesy of the Sam Pillmon family.*

A ticket for one boat ride on the beautiful Chowan River, offered as part of the total entertainment package available to beach patrons. *Frank Stephenson Photo Archives.*

CHOWAN BEACH DISCO EXTRAVAGANZA
ALL-NIGHT DISCO
JULY 15, 1983

FUN AND GAMES   +   CONTEST GALORE
BRING TENTS AND CAMPERS - GATES OPEN 2 pm
invited by
Master Wan & Company

Adults $5.00   Children (under 10) $2.50

Chowan Beach became a favorite stop for disco performers, as seen in this July 15, 1983, ticket to an all night disco jam featuring Master Wan and Company. *Frank Stephenson Photo Archives.*

A poster used to promote Little Freddie Scott, a nationally known recording artist, who appeared at Chowan Beach with The Exciters in the early 1970s. *Frank Stephenson Photo Archives.*

An undated poster advertising The Psychodelic Soul Band. *Frank Stephenson Photo Archives.*

A poster promoting nationally known recording star Eddie Floyd from the late 1970s or early 1980s. *Frank Stephenson Photo Archives.*

Phyllis Pillmon, daughter of Mr. and Mrs. Sam Pillmon, seen with recording star Eddie Floyd during his appearance at Chowan Beach. The photograph dates from the late 1970s or early 1980s and was taken in the restaurant in the beachfront dance hall. *Courtesy of Ms. Phyllis Pillmon.*

The German-made carousel was the signature amusement ride at Chowan Beach. The carousel was in operation until Chowan Beach closed in 1990, due primarily to competition from newly opened amusement parks such as King's Dominion. This 1995 photograph provides a glimpse of the center core of the carousel. *Frank Stephenson Photo Archives.*

Another 1995 view of the carousel. *Frank Stephenson Photo Archives.*

The Chowan Beach carousel, 1995. *Frank Stephenson Photo Archives.*

Many patrons of Chowan Beach stepped up to this booth to purchase tickets for amusement rides. *Frank Stephenson Photo Archives.*

The ravages of time began to take their toll on Chowan Beach, as seen in this 1990s photo of the fun house and dance hall. The pier attached to the right of the dance hall was used to board boats for rides on the Chowan River. *Frank Stephenson Photo Archives.*

This structure was built to house 4-H Club members and other campers who came to Chowan Beach in groups. A few years after the beach closed, it began to deteriorate. *Frank Stephenson Photo Archives.*

Thousands and thousands of excellent dishes were served in the main restaurant at Chowan Beach, pictured here a few years after the beach closed. *Frank Stephenson Photo Archives.*

The beachfront facilities at Chowan Beach a few years after they closed in 1990. *Frank Stephenson Photo Archives.*

1990s view of the covered picnic area on the waterfront at Chowan Beach. *Frank Stephenson Photo Archives.*

1990s view of some of the guest cottages on the waterfront at Chowan Beach. *Frank Stephenson Photo Archives.*

1990s close-up of one of the waterfront guest cottages. *Frank Stephenson Photo Archives.*

1990s view of the waterfront showing the fun house, dance hall, carousel shelter and covered picnic area. *Frank Stephenson Photo Archives.*

1990s view of the original dance hall whose past headliners included B.B. King, James Brown and Ruth Brown. *Frank Stephenson Photo Archives.*

1990s view of one of the guest cottages on the hill at Chowan Beach. African American families would vacation in these guest cottages for a week or two. *Frank Stephenson Photo Archives.*

1990s photo of the carousel and Chowan Beach waterfront. *Frank Stephenson Photo Archives.*

The waterfront concession stand, 1990s. *Frank Stephenson Photo Archives.*

The back of the Reid home and cottages on the waterfront, 1990s. *Frank Stephenson Photo Archives.*

1990s view of the outdoor picnic area on the waterfront at Chowan Beach. This view of the Chowan River is looking south toward Winton, North Carolina. *Frank Stephenson Photo Archives.*

In this 1990s view the beautiful Chowan River slowly but surely takes back the beachfront at Chowan Beach. *Frank Stephenson Photo Archives.*

On September 15, 1999, Hurricane Floyd hit the coast of North Carolina, resulting in severe flooding. The beachfront at Chowan Beach was totally inundated by the waters of the Chowan River. *Frank Stephenson Photo Archives.*

In September 1999 the flood waters from Hurricane Floyd flooded the beachfront dance hall and fun house at Chowan Beach. *Frank Stephenson Photo Archives.*

The greatness and beauty of Chowan Beach still shines in this 1990s view of the waterfront. Chowan Beach was an extraordinary place that was brought to life and fostered and nurtured by two remarkable families, the Eli Reid and Sam Pillmon families of Hertford County, North Carolina. *Frank Stephenson Photo Archives.*